MW01141912

10-Minute Critical-Thinking Activities for English

by

Deborah Eaton

WALCH PUBLISHING

User's Guide
to
Walch Reproducible Books

As part of our general effort to provide educational materials that are as practical and economical as possible, we have designated this publication a "reproducible book." The designation means that purchase of the book includes purchase of the right to limited reproduction of all pages on which this symbol appears:

Here is the basic Walch policy: We grant to individual purchasers of this book the right to make sufficient copies of reproducible pages for use by all students of a single teacher. This permission is limited to a single teacher, and does not apply to entire schools or school systems, so institutions purchasing the book should pass the permission on to a single teacher. Copying of the book or its parts for resale is prohibited.

Any questions regarding this policy or requests to purchase further reproduction rights should be addressed to:

Permissions Editor
J. Weston Walch, Publisher
P. O. Box 658
Portland, Maine 04104-0658

Author Biography

Deborah Eaton has worked in education since 1972 and has been a freelance educational writer for more than 15 years, creating outstanding student texts and teacher materials in reading, writing, and language arts. She has published materials with every major educational publisher in this country, as well as with Berlitz, National Geographic, and Pleasant Company. She is the author of more than 70 classroom storybooks and 2 picture books for young children.

---

1   2   3   4   5   6   7   8   9   10

ISBN 0-8251-3797-7

Copyright © 1998
J. Weston Walch, Publisher
P. O. Box 658 • Portland, Maine 04104-0658
www.walch.com

Printed in the United States of America

Contents

To the Teacher

Here's a way to make every minute in your classroom count. The 56 activities in this book foster logical thinking and inspire independent and creative problem solving, all in a quick 10 minutes.

Use the activities when you are dealing with administrative tasks; use them when you must take some time to focus on one student or a small portion of the class; or use them as a stimulating warm-up, a sure way to sharpen your students' mental focus before launching into the day's lesson.

Designed to appeal to students and support divergent thinking and learning styles, *10-Minute Critical-Thinking Activities for English* provides practice in logical thinking, critical analysis, and creative problem solving. The activities have been created specifically for English classes, and they encourage students to think metaphorically, to make comparisons, inferences, predictions, and judgments. They will enrich your classroom with new approaches to specific language arts topics. Some exercises involve homophones, metaphors, palindromes, anagrams, or word associations. Others demand careful, critical reading.

The activities are divided into four sections. Part 1, *Word Games*, asks students to manipulate language to form new words and word combinations and to apply their language arts knowledge in new ways. Part 2, *Stories to Solve*, requires students to apply strong critical reading and logical thinking skills to answer questions about tricky stories and riddles. In Part 3, *Let's Get Creative*, students must generate lots of alternative ideas for solving problems and creating inventions, as well as describe their ideas adequately in writing. Part 4, *Brain Busters*, is a compendium of puzzles and activities designed to challenge students both to think logically and to be flexible in their approaches to problem solving.

Most of the activities are open-ended; all of them invite a number of problem-solving strategies. Besides honing their own critical thinking skills, students can improve their metacognition—thinking about thinking—by listening to how their classmates go about solving the problems and then adding those strategies to their own problem-solving repertoires.

The activities within each section are presented in random order. No sequence of skills is assumed, so teachers may use any problem in any order. You may use the activity masters to make overhead projections or copies for individual students.

Some of these problems are quite challenging. No students are expected to answer them all correctly—far from it. Part of the goal is to present activities that challenge students to try new problem-solving strategies. And part of the value of critical-thinking puzzles is to share approaches, thereby allowing students to see a number of possible ways to attack any problem. If the problems were not so tricky, they would not be as much fun—or as worthwhile. You may want to post "What to Do When Your Mind Goes Blank" (page viii) to encourage students to persevere.

So take your time on necessary administrative tasks, knowing that your students will be expanding their language arts horizons and becoming better learners with *10-Minute Critical-Thinking Activities for English*.

Enjoy,
Deborah Eaton

Tips on Critical Thinking

Critical-Thinking Questions

You can help your students sharpen their critical-thinking abilities every day. One way to achieve this is to ask the right kinds of questions—probing, open-ended questions that challenge them to think, make connections, use logic, and question their assumptions. Here are some examples of good questions for critical thinking.

How would you categorize the . . . ?

What is the relationship between . . . ?

What evidence can you find that . . . ?

What is the difference between . . . ?

What is the theme?

How would you justify . . . ?

What could you do to improve . . . ?

Can you propose an alternative solution?

What would happen if . . . ?

How do you know . . . ?

What if you combined . . . ?

Can you predict the outcome if . . . ?

What is your theory about why . . . ?

Can you think of an original way to . . . ?

How would you test to see if . . . ?

How would you assess the importance of . . . ?

How would you defend the actions of . . . ?

What do you think of her judgment?

What facts support the conclusion that . . . ?

How would you prioritize . . . ?

Why would anyone choose . . . ?

Would it be better if . . . ?

How would you find out if . . . ?

What does that judgment show about . . . ?

Characteristics of Critical Thinkers

As you assess your students' progress in developing strong logical and critical-thinking strategies, here are some behaviors to consider.

Creative problem solvers . . .

▷ are enthusiastic about problem solving;

▷ persist when challenged—don't give up easily;

▷ relate new problems to ones they have already solved;

▷ try more than one approach or strategy to solve a problem;

▷ can use hints or help to change their attack strategies;

▷ brainstorm to get started;

▷ organize information in helpful ways;

▷ take risks and propose ideas beyond the routine and conventional;

▷ make interesting or unusual associations and connections;

▷ are flexible—willing to try different approaches in different situations;

▷ combine things they know in new ways;

▷ are willing to consider new viewpoints on a problem;

▷ organize information logically and can spot inconsistencies;

▷ examine their own thinking processes and can explain their method for solving a problem.

The
Activities

Matrix of Critical-Thinking Skills

Page No.	ACTIVITY	Language Applications	Logical Reasoning	Associative Thinking	Creative Thinking	Creative Fluency	Analysis	Critical Reading	Writing	Synthesis	Evaluation and Making Judgments
2	Word Squares	✔									
3	A Picture Is Worth . . .	✔			✔		✔				
4	Common Knowledge			✔							
5	Double Trouble	✔		✔							
6	Decomposition	✔									
7	You've Got a Pal . . .	✔									
8	More Word Pictures	✔			✔		✔				
9	Alice, Lice, Lie	✔	✔								
10	Word Bits	✔									
11	Word Chains	✔									
12	Not Baaad!	✔		✔		✔					
13	Word Follow-ups	✔		✔							
14	Vocabulary Stretches	✔		✔		✔					
15	A-Maze-Ing						✔		✔		
17	Nab the Kidnapper!		✔				✔	✔			
18	The Fibber		✔				✔	✔			
19	The Cookie Monster		✔				✔	✔			
20	The Motorcycle in . . .		✔				✔	✔			
21	A Crabby Cabby		✔				✔	✔			
22	Food Chain Farmer		✔				✔	✔			
23	Taradiddle		✔				✔	✔			
24	Meow Times Four		✔				✔				
25	The Draggin' Dragons		✔				✔	✔			
26	Nightmare		✔				✔	✔			
28	What If???				✔		✔				✔
29	Not to Decide . . .						✔				✔
30	Look out Below!				✔	✔	✔		✔		✔

(continued)

Matrix of Critical-Thinking Skills *(continued)*

Page No.	Activity	Language Applications	Logical Reasoning	Associative Thinking	Creative Thinking	Creative Fluency	Analysis	Critical Reading	Writing	Synthesis	Evaluation and Making Judgments
31	Forever				✔	✔	✔				✔
32	Recycle Challenge				✔	✔				✔	
33	Dictionary Madness	✔		✔	✔					✔	
34	Shrink and Stretch				✔		✔			✔	
35	Peek Pocket				✔	✔				✔	
36	Eggsactly				✔		✔		✔	✔	
37	Peanut Butter Is . . .			✔	✔		✔				
38	What Kind of Animal . . .	✔		✔			✔				
39	No Lion Around				✔	✔				✔	
40	Imogene Ashun's . . .	✔		✔			✔				
41	Splat the Blats				✔		✔			✔	✔
42	A Pungent Problem				✔		✔			✔	✔
43	You Name It	✔		✔	✔					✔	
45	Hidden Animals	✔		✔		✔					
46	Bow Wow Wower		✔				✔	✔			
47	A Problem with Poetry				✔		✔	✔	✔		
48	Proverbial Wisdom	✔	✔				✔				
49	New World		✔				✔				✔
50	Egghead Nursery Rhymes	✔					✔	✔	✔		
51	Super Egghead . . .	✔		✔			✔	✔			
52	Unmentionables	✔			✔		✔		✔		
53	Burn, Baby, Burn						✔		✔		✔
54	Common Threads	✔		✔							
55	Above or Below?		✔				✔			✔	
56	Traditional Riddles		✔		✔		✔				
57	Hink Pinks	✔		✔	✔						
58	Letter Soup	✔	✔	✔							
59	Don't Bug Me		✔				✔				
60	Word Associations	✔		✔						✔	

What to Do When Your Mind Goes Blank

1. Take a deep breath and refuse to be confused; go back over the problem one step at a time.

2. Organize what you know on paper.

3. Act the problem out in your mind.

4. Doodle—move things into new combinations.

5. Make a graph or a table or a diagram.

6. Work the problem backwards.

7. Solve part of the problem.

8. Look for a pattern.

9. Ask "What if . . . ?" and follow that reasoning through.

10. Brainstorm: Even silly ideas can lead to something helpful.

11. Don't give up.

12. Don't give up.

13. Don't give up.

14. Don't give up.

15. Don't give up.

10-Minute Critical-Thinking Activities for English

PART 1: Word Games

These word games emphasize logical thinking and give students an opportunity to apply what they know about language and language arts rules in unusual ways. Students will break words down into their component parts, recombine letters and words to build new words, stretch their vocabulary, and make associations among words and phrases.

Encourage students to keep at it if they don't immediately see the answers to a puzzle. Part of the goal is to wrestle with the puzzles, experiment, and try new thinking strategies.

You may want to point out that experience is an important factor to success in this kind of word manipulation and "puzzle think." Some students may initially be more apt than others at these word games, but all of them will benefit from the practice.

Those of your students who are already "puzzle masters" can use their extra time to make up more puzzle items of a similar type.

Word Squares

Fill in the squares below to make words. All the squares in a row must be filled. You may use your dictionary, a textbook, or any other reference.

Scoring 1 point for each completed word
1 extra point for each word that is related to science,
  social studies, or music
5 extra points if all words are somehow related
2 points off for any misspelled word

| S | | | | | | | | |

| | | | | S |

| T | | | | | | |

| M | | | |

| | | | | R |

My Score

Words completed _____ × 1 point = _____

Words related to science/social studies/music:

_____ × 1 point = _____

Are all words related? How? _____ = <u>5 points</u>

Words misspelled _____ × 2 = _____ (subtract)

My total score is _____.

(Maximum score = 15)

Name _____ Date _____

A Picture Is Worth at Least a Couple of Words

These picture puzzles represent common expressions. Solve them. Write what each one means under the picture. Then make up three of your own.

|R E A D I N G| _reading between_ _the lines_	**man** _____ _____	**GROUND** _____ _____
gra snake ss _____ _____	I N L O V E _____ _____	**CHAIR** _____ _____
  _____ _____	 _____ _____	 _____ _____

Common Knowledge

Each pair below has a word in common. The first letter of each answer is given. Fill in the common word.

1. swimming and card games

    <u>s</u> <u>u</u> <u>i</u> <u>t</u> <u>s</u>

2. figure skating and refrigerator

    <u>i</u> __ __

3. baseball and bowling

    <u>s</u> __ __ __ __ __

4. basketball and fishing

    <u>n</u> __ __

5. auto races and train station

    <u>t</u> __ __ __ __

6. ballroom dancing and ice cream store

    <u>d</u> __ __ __

7. baseball and jewelry store

    <u>d</u> __ __ __ __ __ __

8. sailing and card games

    <u>d</u> __ __ __

9. golf and playground

    <u>s</u> __ __ __ __

10. deer hunting and wallets

    <u>b</u> __ __ __ __

10-Minute Critical-Thinking Activities for English

Double Trouble

Homophones are words that sound the same but have different spellings and different meanings. Finish each sentence below by filling in the blanks with homophones.

Example: If your soup gets cold, you'll have to eat <u>chilly chili</u>.

1. I dug a pit in the yard, but dad made me fill in the _____ _____.

2. The patient asked the foot doctor, "Will my _____ _____ ?"

3. Neighing all day might make a _____ _____.

4. The 12-year-old gold prospector was a _____ _____.

5. If our garden was overgrown with grass, _____ _____ it.

6. Steel would not burn in our fireplace, but _____ _____.

7. Little Bambi the fawn is a _____ _____.

8. A white bucket is a _____ _____.

9. I can't see the skunk, but my _____ _____ it is there.

10. The cookies were so delicious that I _____ _____ of them.

11. Our chickens and ducks smell so bad we call them _____ _____.

12. There are bargains at the boat store during the _____ _____.

13. The bank granted just one mortgage; it was their _____ _____.

14. When the people in the waiting room got tired of waiting, the doctor said,

    "Please have some _____, _____ !"

15. Mom's clock said 1:57, and mine said three minutes _____ _____,

    _____.

5

Decomposition

Take these words apart, one letter at a time. Each time you remove a letter, the remaining letters must spell a word. Watch out! You may have to change the order of the letters.

riders

rider

ride

rid

id

I

barbed	salmon	pastry
_ _ _ _ _	_ _ _ _ _	_ _ _ _ _
_ _ _ _	_ _ _ _	_ _ _ _
_ _ _	_ _ _	_ _ _
_ _	_ _	_ _
_	_	_

planter	steamer	rasping
_ _ _ _ _ _	_ _ _ _ _ _	_ _ _ _ _ _
_ _ _ _ _	_ _ _ _ _	_ _ _ _ _
_ _ _ _	_ _ _ _	_ _ _ _
_ _ _	_ _ _	_ _ _
_ _	_ _	_ _
_	_	_

You've Got a Pal in Palindrome

A *palindrome* is a word or phrase that reads the same backwards as forwards. "Madam, I'm Adam" is a palindrome.

How many smaller words can you find in the word *palindrome?* There are more than 80, so good luck! *Hint:* Feel free to scramble the letters!

PALINDROME

More Word Pictures

These picture puzzles represent common expressions. Solve them. Write what each one means under the picture. Then make up three of your own.

NI4NI A2th4A2th	*(pen crossed with sword)*	*(HAIRS with circle and slash)*
g n i p Jones e Jones e k	she she she *(curved line)*	e safety l safety k safety c safety u b
WORKING HAHANDND	*(weather map of U.S.)* feeling	÷ and conquer

Name _____   Date _____

Alice, Lice, Lie

Lewis Carroll, the author of *Alice in Wonderland* and *Alice Through the Looking Glass,* invented this game. It's called *Doublets.* To solve a doublet, you change one word into another, one letter at a time. Each time you change a letter, you must form a real word.

Example: must

                 mast

                 cast

                 can't

Watch out! You will have to switch the order of the letters to solve some of these doublets.

1. WARM
   _____
   _____
   _____
   COLD

2. LOSE
   _____
   _____
   _____
   FIND

3. MORE
   _____
   _____
   _____
   LESS

4. NONE
   _____
   _____
   SOME

5. HARD
   _____
   _____
   _____
   _____
   SOFT

6. SHOW
   _____
   _____
   _____
   _____
   _____
   TELL

Word Bits

Put together two of the three-letter word bits to form a word in the category listed. Write the word.

1. Animals	SAL	CAT	KET	RAC	TLE	_____
2. Trees	WAL	TER	LET	NUT	RUS	_____
3. Food	FET	CAR	FIN	ISH	MUF	_____
4. Colors	COB	GRE	PLE	BRO	PUR	_____
5. Stories	TAL	FOL	END	LEG	FAB	_____
6. Storms	TOR	EZE	ALL	PLE	SQU	_____
7. Careers	OUT	DOC	YER	LAW	TUR	_____
8. Tools	HAM	CHI	ECT	LLY	SEL	_____
9. Body Part	FOO	GER	FIN	ISH	MAN	_____
10. Numbers	SEV	FIF	VEN	IAL	ELE	_____
11. Music	LIN	TRU	TLE	VIO	PET	_____
12. Money	DOL	KEL	CAS	NIC	DIM	_____
13. Places	MOU	FOR	ERT	DES	SWA	_____
14. Feelings	SAD	RET	REG	GOR	ANG	_____
15. Birds	ROB	KEY	BLE	TUR	IRD	_____

Word Chains

Make word chains. Put in the brackets three letters that will complete the first word and begin the next. Here's an example:

Example: ICI [<u>CLE</u>] VER (icicle and clever)

1. BAS [   ] TLE

2. COL [   ] GER

3. LET [   ] ROR

4. PEP [   ] ISH

5. MAS [   ] TON

6. SUD [   ] TAL

7. RAS [   ] ICO

8. PUC [   ] NEL

9. HAR [   ] DER

10. WEA [   ] DER

Did you finish quickly?

Make up a word chain of your own below.

_____

Not Baaad!

Onomatopoeia is the use of words that imitate natural sounds, such as <u>woof</u> or <u>toot</u>. See if you can be the onomatopoeia champ. Can you write 45 onomatopoetic words?

_____   _____   _____

_____   _____   _____

_____   _____   _____

_____   _____   _____

_____   _____   _____

_____   _____   _____

_____   _____   _____

_____   _____   _____

_____   _____   _____

_____   _____   _____

_____   _____   _____

_____   _____   _____

_____   _____   _____

_____   _____   _____

_____   _____   _____

Name _____   Date _____

Word Follow-ups

One word can be added to the word trios below to make sense as a compound noun or phrase with each word. Add the word that belongs.

Examples: child, neighbor, sister   <u>hood</u>

                     radio, fire, gas   <u>station</u>

1. sea, nut, bomb   _____

2. fire, country, bed   _____

3. scholar, town, member   _____

4. high, door, run   _____

5. soft, sore, hot   _____

6. tom, copy, fat   _____

7. fire, stone, blank   _____

8. bird, hen, doll   _____

9. safe, fire, soda   _____

10. shopping, tea, hand   _____

Vocabulary Stretches

Write as many words as you can think of in each category.

Synonyms or Near-Synonyms for *Said*	Synonyms or Near-Synonyms for *Walk*	Words Describing *Emotions*

Name _____ Date _____

A-Maze-Ing

I n just 10 minutes, your best friend will be blindfolded and thrust into the dreaded
Swamp Maze. Only you can help your friend get through the maze safely. Quickly!
Write the instructions your friend will need to survive.

_____

_____

_____

_____

_____

PART 2: Stories to Solve

Critical thinking is always essential to understanding what we read. These activities give students practice in critical analysis—examining information, making comparisons, identifying inconsistencies, making inferences, and finding evidence to support them.

The stories are tricky. After all, they were written with the intention of confusing or misleading. Encourage your students to be persistent. One characteristic of a good problem solver is a refusal to give up. Point out that no one will solve all the problems. The goal here is to face a challenge logically and creatively and not to give in. Instruct students to list everything they know about the problem on the page if they cannot find the key to solving a story.

These activities are the ones most likely to frustrate some students. You may want to post "What to Do When Your Mind Goes Blank" to encourage students to keep trying. If possible, set aside a few minutes to discuss how each problem could be solved. Thinking about thinking and hearing other approaches are both great practice for critical thinkers.

Nab the Kidnapper!

Richie Fullpockets, high school senior, was kidnapped! A ransom note demanded that his family pay $250,000 "or else!"

The Fullpockets family paid the ransom. Richie was found, blindfolded, and tied to a chair in a local warehouse. Luckily, he was unharmed. He told the police that he had been attacked from behind. He never even saw the kidnapper.

The police moved quickly. They picked up two suspicious men in the area.

The first suspect, Johnny Misdemeanor, claimed he was walking through the neighborhood on his way to his sister's house. He saw no one he knew. No one could confirm his whereabouts. But he demanded to be put in a lineup immediately, so his name could be cleared.

The second suspect, Harry Lightfingers, said he was in the area but swore he didn't do it. He said he got lost looking for the nearest subway station. He said he asked a passerby for directions but couldn't describe him. Harry wanted to take a lie detector test right away to prove he didn't do it.

One suspect is the kidnapper. Which is it, Johnny or Harry?

How do you know?

_____

_____

_____

_____

_____

_____

_____

The Fibber

Barney Fibber called the police to report a burglary.

Detective Finemind answered the call and arrived on the scene.

"What did they steal?" he asked.

"All my wife's jewelry, the TV, VCR, CD player, and computer," Barney told him. "All the big-ticket items. They got in through this window," he explained.

The window did look as though it had been jimmied.

The two men went outside to examine it. Sure enough, the bottom of the window frame was scraped and scratched. A crowbar lay on the ground.

"Hey, that's my crowbar," Barney Fibber said. "That belongs in the garage."

"Are the stolen items insured?" Detective Finemind asked.

"Oh, yes," Barney answered. "That's the only good thing about all this."

"Did they take any big items from the garage?" the detective asked. "Lawn mower? Power tools?"

"Nope," said Barney. "The door's still locked. It doesn't even look as though they went in there."

"Sorry, Mr. Fibber," said Finemind, getting out his handcuffs. "I'm going to have to arrest you for fraud. You robbed yourself, didn't you?"

How did Detective Finemind know that Barney Fibber was the burglar?

_____

_____

_____

_____

_____

_____

Name_____ Date _____

The Cookie Monster

Who stole the cookies from the cookie jar? Remember that old game? Well, now you can figure out who really did take those cookies. Read the statements below. Only one is true.

     Margaret: "Susan took the cookies from the cookie jar."

     Susan: "Katherine took the cookies."

     Debbie: "Who, me? No way."

     Katherine: "Susan is lying when she says I took that cookie."

So who took those cookies? _____

How do you know?

_____

_____

_____

_____

_____

_____

_____

_____

(Okay, okay, here's a hint: Look at each person's statement. If that statement is true, what about the others?)

The Motorcycle in the Dell

Two brothers wanted their dad's old leather motorcycle jacket. They argued and argued, but they just couldn't agree on which one of them should have it.

"Tell you what," their dad said, "Why don't you race for it? I'll give my jacket to the brother whose motorcycle reaches Sunny Dell *last*."

The brothers agreed to race, but neither could figure out how to make sure he was the last to get to the finish line. They hung around in the driveway all day, watching each other, but neither made a move toward his motorcycle.

Their dad waited and waited for the race to begin.

"Well," he said finally, "I guess I'll have to give you a hint about how to win this race." He leaned over and whispered something in the younger brother's ear.

"Oh! Right!" said the younger brother. He jumped onto a motorcycle and raced toward Sunny Dell just as fast as he could go. The other brother followed just as quickly. The race was on!

What did the father whisper into his son's ear?

_____

_____

_____

_____

_____

A Crabby Cabby

A man hailed a taxi in Chicago. He was on vacation and having a great time. On the way to his destination, the airport, he talked and talked, telling the taxi driver about all the sights he'd seen and the places he'd visited on his trip.

The taxi driver was in a very bad mood. Finally, he couldn't take any more jabbering.

"I'm sorry, mister," he yelled. "I'm deaf, and my hearing aid battery died. I can't hear a single word you are saying!"

That shut the man up.

The taxi driver breathed a sigh of relief.

The man arrived at his destination and paid his fare. When he was boarding his plane, however, he suddenly realized that the taxi driver had been lying.

How did he know?

_____

_____

_____

_____

_____

_____

_____

Food Chain Farmer

A farmer was traveling home with a fox, a chicken, and a sack of corn. He had to be very careful. The fox was always trying to eat the chicken, and the chicken couldn't wait to get at that sack of corn.

On the way, the farmer came to a river. He had to use a rowboat to cross the river. But the boat was only big enough to fit himself and one of the items he was carrying at a time. He was going to have to do a lot of rowing!

How could the farmer safely get all his possessions across the river?

_____

_____

_____

_____

_____

_____

_____

_____

_____

_____

Taradiddle

On the South Sea isle of Taradiddle live two kinds of incredible talking birds. The Veritees always, always tell the truth. The Whoppers invariably lie. Unfortunately, it's almost impossible to tell the two birds apart on sight.

A vacationer on Taradiddle was trying to find his way back to the Grass Hut Hotel when he came upon two birds. The first bird was in a tree. The second bird was on the ground.

"Are you a Veritee?" the tourist asked the bird in the tree.

"He'll say yes, but he'll be lying," said the bird on the ground.

Which bird was a Veritee, and which was a Whopper? How do you know?

_____

_____

_____

_____

_____

_____

_____

_____

_____

(*Hint*: Think about it—the bird in the tree would say "yes" in any case.)

Meow Times Four

The animal control officer rounded up four stray cats: Pudge, Purdue, Piglet, and Mr. Kitty. He put them each in a cage, and the four cages were in a row.

Pudge's cage is next to Purdue's.

But Pudge's cage is not next to Piglet's.

If Piglet's cage is not next to Mr. Kitty's, whose is? _____

(*Hint*: Diagram it!)

The Draggin' Dragons

Once upon a fairy tale, four dragons named Flame, Smoke, Fangs, and Grumpy were laying waste to the countryside. The princess, who had been granted 10 wishes at birth, decided to use 4 of them to rid the land of the destructive dragons. She turned one into a mouse, one into a flea, one into a kitten, and the last into a handsome gerbil.

Flame was not the mouse and not the flea.

Smoke was not the kitten or the mouse.

If Flame was not the kitten, then Fangs was not the mouse.

Grumpy was neither the flea nor the mouse.

Fangs was not the flea or the kitten.

What animal was each dragon changed into?

Flame was a _____ .

Fangs was a _____ .

Smoke was a _____ .

Grumpy was a _____ .

(*Hint*: Draw a grid to keep track of what you know.)

Nightmare

Long ago in a faraway land, a guard stood night watch over King Enslow's palace. One night, he had a terrible nightmare.

The guard dreamed that his king was killed in a dastardly plot and that the terrible deed would take place at a boar hunt the very next morning. The guard hurried to his king and told him about the dream.

After pondering on what he had heard, King Enslow thanked the guard and assured him he would avoid the boar hunt. Then he called the head of all the palace guards and ordered that the night guard be beheaded immediately.

Why would the king do such a thing?

_____

_____

_____

_____

_____

_____

PART 3: Let's Get Creative

Good critical thinkers try out new ideas and propose alternate solutions that look at a problem in a new way. Part of creating this flexibility of outlook and willingness to take risks with new ideas is practicing the art of brainstorming and stretching one's imagination.

The activities in this section are creativity stretchers. Many of the problems are unusual or outlandish. To solve them, students must go beyond their usual analytical and logical outlooks and try something new. By asking students to generate many ideas or make metaphorical connections or design unusual inventions, these activities encourage creative problem solving. The goal is to develop creative thinking by encouraging fluency (the generation of many ideas or plans), flexibility (a variety of approaches to a problem), and originality.

If students get stuck on these activities, encourage them to look at things differently, turn the page upside down, think of the silliest or largest or smallest thing they can, and try a new approach to the problem.

What If???

What if animals could talk? Think about it. Then list 10 ways our world would probably be different as a result.

1. _____

_____

2. _____

_____

3. _____

_____

4. _____

_____

5. _____

_____

6. _____

_____

7. _____

_____

8. _____

_____

9. _____

_____

10. _____

_____

Name _____   Date _____

Not to Decide Is to Decide

There are lots of different kinds of decision makers. Read about each one. Then write a *pro* and a *con* for each decision-making style.

1. The "Not yet!" decision maker. This person always waits until the very last minute to make a decision.

   pro _____

   con _____

2. The "It's a cinch!" decision maker. This person makes decisions easily, just choosing what looks easiest or simplest.

   pro _____

   con _____

3. The "Complicated" decision maker. This person sees so many possibilities! He or she looks at every possible angle to even the smallest questions.

   pro _____

   con _____

4. The "What do you think?" decision maker. This person always asks someone else for an opinion.

   pro _____

   con _____

5. The "Aggressive" decision maker. This person makes a decision fast, then goes all out for it.

   pro _____

   con _____

What kind of decision maker are you? What kind would you like to be? Why?

_____

_____

_____

Look out Below!

Aliens are hovering in their spacecraft above planet Earth. They don't look very friendly. In fact, their laser guns are pointed right at us here below. Their leader has demanded that we earthlings send up a letter and some photographs proving that we deserve to live. Then they will decide whether to annihilate us. You are the lucky person who will write that letter and choose the photos. What will you do?

Excerpts from my letter:

_____

_____

_____

_____

_____

_____

_____

Descriptions of some of my photos:

_____

_____

_____

_____

Forever

Abright light shines in your bedroom window. You blink, and lose all sense of time. The next thing you know, you are in a large, featureless room. A voice says, "Welcome, Chosen One." The voice informs you that you will now live forever but that you must remain in this room. It directs you to fill out a list of 20 items to have with you in the room. Clearly, the owner of the voice has strange powers. You may have whatever you wish. What will be on your list?

1. _____
2. _____
3. _____
4. _____
5. _____
6. _____
7. _____
8. _____
9. _____
10. _____
11. _____
12. _____
13. _____
14. _____
15. _____
16. _____
17. _____
18. _____
19. _____
20. _____

Name _____   Date _____

Recycle Challenge

We throw a lot of things away every day. But they say that one person's trash is another person's treasure. Think of ways to reuse these common items together in one project. Draw your idea. Write a three-line ad that describes it.

1. A newspaper
2. Old gift wrap
3. An empty coffee can

4. Used tinfoil
5. An empty ballpoint pen

_____

_____

_____

Dictionary Madness

Did you know? *Yelly* is something they use on peanut butter sandwiches in Sweden. And a broken ornament in the shape of an angel is called a *dangle*. Make up words for these definitions and definitions for these words.

1. A rodeo for chickens is called a _____.

2. A piece of food caught between your teeth is a _____.

3. A back scratcher for elephants is a _____.

4. When you sing pop rock in the shower, you are _____.

5. Boiled grasshoppers with chocolate sauce taste _____.

6. A *blurtain* is _____

   _____.

7. When you *prissyclunk*, you are really _____

   _____.

8. A *flister* is a _____

   _____.

9. Something is *flibbinought* when it _____

   _____.

10. You can *deggin* when _____

   _____.

Shrink and Stretch

A vacuum cleaner, if it were shrunk, could be used to clean up crumbs from the dining room table. Write one or more ideas about how to use each of these things.

If they were shrunk

1. A washing machine _____

   _____

2. A shovel _____

   _____

3. A skateboard _____

   _____

4. A basketball hoop_____

   _____

5. Your math teacher _____

   _____

If they were much larger

6. A jogging shoe _____

   _____

7. A mouse trap_____

   _____

8. A compact disc _____

   _____

9. A comb _____

   _____

10. A butterfly_____

    _____

Name _____   Date _____

Peek Pocket

Yipes! There's a mouse peeking out of your back pocket. You want to get rid of the little pest, of course. Unfortunately, your hands are tied together in front of you right now. List 15 ways you could get the mouse out of your pocket—without injuring it. Be creative!

1. _____

2. _____

3. _____

4. _____

5. _____

6. _____

7. _____

8. _____

9. _____

10. _____

11. _____

12. _____

13. _____

14. _____

15. _____

                   10-Minute Critical-Thinking Activities for English

Name _____   Date _____

Eggsactly

This hen will lay eggs only in a nest with a hole in the bottom. Design a device that will safely catch each egg and move it out of the way before the next egg is laid. Draw your device. Tell how it works.

My invention is called a _____.

Here's how it works: _____

_____

_____

_____

_____

_____

36   *10-Minute Critical-Thinking Activities for English*

Name _____ Date _____

Peanut Butter Is the Center of the Universe

Petey Tubber loves peanut butter. In fact, he swears that everything in the universe is related to peanut butter in some way or other. For example, rocks are like peanut butter. Some rocks are smooth and some are bumpy, just as some peanut butter is smooth and some is chunky. Clapping is like peanut butter, too. A clap always goes between two hands, and peanut butter goes between two slices of bread.

Tell one way each of the following things is like peanut butter. (It's okay to be a little silly, as long as you make a connection.)

1. Fish _____

   _____

2. Rugs _____

   _____

3. Socks _____

   _____

4. Chickadees _____

   _____

5. Walls _____

   _____

6. Eggs _____

   _____

7. Dogs _____

   _____

8. Moon _____

   _____

9. Worms _____

   _____

10. Stamps _____

   _____

Name _____   Date _____

What Kind of Animal Is Your Uncle?

Sometimes you can tell a lot about people by comparing them to something else. Here are some examples:

> If my sister were a color, it would be red because she's always so loud and so angry.

> If that politician were a musical instrument, he'd be a bagpipe because he's full of hot air.

Choose a famous person or someone you know very well. Use this technique to describe him or her.

What color is this person? Why? _____

_____

What animal is this person? Why? _____

_____

What plant? Why? _____

_____

What piece of clothing? Why? _____

_____

What toy? Why? _____

_____

What food? Why? _____

_____

What sport? Why? _____

_____

What weather? Why? _____

_____

No Lion Around

List 10 ways to saddle an angry lion. Your ideas may be practical or silly, but be sure to try a number of different approaches!

1. _____
_____

2. _____
_____

3. _____
_____

4. _____
_____

5. _____
_____

6. _____
_____

7. _____
_____

8. _____
_____

9. _____
_____

10. _____
_____

Imogene Ashun's Quotations

I magine who might have said each of these quotations—and in what situation. Your answers may be serious or silly.

Example: "I have nothing to offer but blood, sweat, and tears."

<u>The high school quarterback who forgot to bring the ball to the big game.</u>

1. "We must learn to live together as brothers, or we will perish together as fools."

    _____

    _____

2. "A journey of a thousand miles must begin with one step." _____

    _____

3. "I never forget a face, but in your case I'll make an exception." _____

    _____

4. "I could write the saddest poem tonight." _____

    _____

5. "Speak softly but carry a big stick." _____

    _____

6. "It was a bright, cold day in April, and the clocks were striking thirteen."

    _____

    _____

7. "East is East and West is West and never the twain shall meet." _____

    _____

Splat the Blats

The poor Blands have no hands, and the pesky Blats are biting like gnats. Help the Blands protect themselves from those irritating little insects. Draw an invention the Blands can take with them when they are outside to protect their sensitive skin. Label it to show how it works.

A Pungent Problem

Uh-oh. Somehow you've caught a skunk in your special, patented Heart-Kind trap. The skunk is unharmed, but it can't get out. It's up to you to help it. Draw your solution and write about how it works. Oh—by the way—skunks can spray their noxious scent five feet away!

_____

_____

_____

_____

_____

You Name It

Do you know Warren Peace? (He just wrote a LONG book.)
Belle E. Laugh? (She knows lots of great jokes.)
Otto Mobile? (He really gets around.)
Justin Time? (He's never late.)
Make up some funny names of your own. Write something about each one, like the comments in the parentheses above, to show who they are or what they do. To get started, look at the names and initials in the box.

I. M.	B.	Cary
O. U.	Billy	U. R.
Phil	Candy	B. A.

Name   **Description**

_____   _____

_____   _____

_____   _____

_____   _____

_____   _____

_____   _____

_____   _____

_____   _____

_____   _____

_____   _____

PART 4: Brain Busters

This section contains puzzlers and stumpers of all kinds. The activities challenge students to use many different skills, including logical thinking, analysis, synthesis, and evaluation. Besides more traditional and nontraditional puzzles, some activities here challenge students to evaluate complex situations and make judgments based on their own knowledge and values. The value of these activities will be increased tremendously by the sharing of approaches, ideas, and judgments, since an important part of critical thinking involves evaluating new or different ideas.

If you feel an individual activity is particularly challenging for your students, you may want to organize the class into pairs or teams. Sharing brainstorming and problem-solving approaches is invaluable in developing critical-thinking abilities.

Hidden Animals

The word match for each definition below contains the same three-letter animal name. Write your answers, one letter to a line. You may use a dictionary or thesaurus, if necessary.

1. __ __ __ __ __   Very pale

2. __ __ __ __ __ __ __ __   A place of culinary pursuits

3. __ __ __ __ __ __ __   It looks like moss and grows on rocks.

4. __ __ __ __   Not now

5. __ __ __ __ __ __ __ __ __   A bedspread or bathrobe fabric

6. __ __ __ __ __ __   A city in Greece

7. __ __ __ __ __ __ __ __   Pagan or barbarous

8. __ __ __ __ __   A reddish plant dye

Bonus: How many words can you think of that contain the letters *cat?*

_____   _____   _____

_____   _____   _____

_____   _____   _____

_____   _____   _____

       10-Minute Critical-Thinking Activities for English

Bow Wow Wower

Emily, Bret, Brandon, Sandy, and Rosie have dogs that they love. The dogs' names are Bruiser, Fiddle, Ralph, Snooky, and Sam. All the dogs are different breeds. There's a collie, a spaniel, a terrier, a poodle, and a basset hound. Use the clues below to figure out the name and breed of each kid's dog. Put X's for "no" and O's for "yes" on the graphs to keep track of what you know.

1. Ralph is neither Bret's nor Sandy's dog.

2. No dog's name begins with the same letter as his owner's name.

3. Sam's owner and the owner of the spaniel have names that begin with the same letter.

4. Snooky is not a basset; neither are Emily's nor Brandon's dogs.

5. Bret's dog and the collie are NOT Sam or Snooky.

6. Rosie's dog is not a terrier.

	Bruiser	Fiddle	Ralph	Snooky	Sam
Emily					
Bret					
Brandon					
Sandy					
Rosie					

	collie	spaniel	terrier	poodle	basset hound
Bruiser					
Fiddle					
Ralph					
Snooky					
Sam					

(Hint: Once you have a circle, you can put X's in all the other boxes in that line.)

A Problem with Poetry

E mily Dickinson wrote these poems. Too bad the typist left one word out of each one! Read each poem. Use your dictionary to look up any words that are new to you. Then add the word you think might be missing. Explain why you chose that word.

Poem 1

_____ is the thing with feathers
That perches in the soul,
And sings the tune without the words,
And never stops at all.

And sweetest in the gale is heard;
And sore must be the storm
That could abash the little bird
That kept so many warm.

I've heard it in the chilliest land
And on the strangest sea;
Yet, never, in extremity,
It asked a crumb of me.

Why I chose my word:

Poem 2

I dwell in _____
A fairer home than Prose,
More numerous of windows,
Superior of doors.

Of chambers, as the cedars—
Impregnable of eye;
And for an everlasting roof
The gables of the sky.

Of visitors—the fairest—
For occupation—this—
The spreading wide my narrow hands
To gather Paradise.

Poem 1

_____

_____

_____

_____

_____

_____

Poem 2

_____

_____

_____

_____

_____

_____

Proverbial Wisdom

Can you break the code and read the message below? Sure you can. Here's how: Look for patterns and for small, common words. Think about where vowels usually fall in our words. Using a pencil, lightly write your guesses above the coded letters in the message. Keep track of your solved letters in the alphabet. Once you have cracked the code, write your message below.

Z DRHV NZM NZB XSZMTV SRH NRMW; Z ULLO, MVEVI.

A B C D E F G H I J K L M N O P Q R S T U V W X Y Z

The message is:

_____

_____

Did you crack the code really fast?
Now make up your own code, and encode a message for a friend to solve.

Name_____   Date _____

New World

Congratulations! You are in complete charge of the country. A brilliant scientist has just perfected the long-awaited antiaging pill, and you must decide how it is to be used. The pill is very, very expensive. And world population is still growing by leaps and bounds. Come on. It's time to formulate your rules for this new product.

1. Who will be allowed to have the pill? Just healthy people? People who can afford it? Just smart people? Will criminals be allowed to have it? Will you share it with people in other countries?

   _____

   _____

   _____

   _____

2. At what age will people be allowed to take the pill? Why?

   _____

   _____

3. Will you control population growth? How?

   _____

   _____

4. What do you think might happen to the economy as a result of the introduction of this pill? Why?

   _____

   _____

   _____

5. Do you think an antiaging pill is a good thing or not? Why?

   _____

   _____

   _____

Egghead Nursery Rhymes

Egbert Egghead can write only in big, fancy words. Here's the way he tells a favorite nursery rhyme. Can you add the title?

A trio of visually impaired diminutive rodents! Observe the manner in which they advance with prodigious rapidity. The entire aggregate pursued the agricultural engineer's spouse, who severed their hindmost protuberances with a keen-edged instrument designed for slicing animal flesh. Has the current reader ever observed such a singular occurrence in his or her animated span of existence as a trio of visually impaired diminutive rodents?

Now write your own "Egghead Nursery Rhyme." Choose a short one! (Possibilities include "Little Boy Blue," "Jack Sprat," "Hey Diddle Diddle," or "Humpty Dumpty.")

_____

_____

_____

_____

_____

_____

_____

_____

_____

_____

_____

_____

Super Egghead Proverbs

Rewrite each proverb below in "regular" language. You might discover a few you recognize! (You may use a dictionary if you need to.)

1. Each cumulonimbus mass of visible vapor contains an interior facing with a chromelike surface.

   _____

2. It is a noxious draft of moving current that conveys benevolence to not one homo sapiens.

   _____

3. What is liquid flavoring for the female domesticated, web-footed, honking, egg-laying, winged vertebrate is liquid flavoring for the male domesticated, web-footed, honking, egg-laying winged vertebrate.

   _____

4. Light precipitation in the fourth month of the calendar year conveys as a consequence the appearance of clusters of the reproductive structures of plants in the fifth month of the same calendar year.

   _____

5. Egotistic vanity goes in advance of a vertical drop from a higher to a lower position.

   _____

6. An intimate companion during a state of want or deficiency is in truth an intimate companion.

   _____

7. If you assume a recumbent position with four-footed, domesticated, carnivorous mammals of the canine family, you will arise in the company of small, wingless, blood-sucking insects.

   _____

8. The residential abode of a person or family is the location of the primary organ of the circulatory system.

   _____

9. The appearance of physical pulchritude is as shallow as a membranous body covering.

   _____

10. Where there is the by-product of the combustion of organic substances, there is the light and heat that results from the oxidation of fuel.

    _____

Unmentionables

Write a paragraph for each story below, following the instructions.
Try to make your writing sound natural, not stiff!

1. During the family camping trip, they cooked hot dogs on sticks over the campfire. Describe it without using any form of the words *campfire, hot dog, sticks,* or
   cooked.

   _____

   _____

   _____

   _____

2. Mom is bringing little Erik's new baby sister home from the hospital today. Tell
   about the occasion without using any form of *hospital, baby, sister,* or *home.*

   _____

   _____

   _____

   _____

3. Nathan is very nervous. He's waiting for Brittany outside the school. Today is the
   day he's going to ask her to the Harvest Dance. Describe what happens without
   using any form of *date, school, ask,* or *dance.*

   _____

   _____

   _____

   _____

Burn, Baby, Burn

Imagine you are a wooden kitchen match, lying in a box on the kitchen counter. Will someone use you soon to light a candle? burn a love note? sterilize a needle? Who knows?

Write three reasons why you do **not** want anyone to light you.

1. _____

   _____

2. _____

   _____

3. _____

   _____

Now write three reasons why you **do** possibly want to be lit.

1. _____

   _____

2. _____

   _____

3. _____

   _____

Write a short description of what might happen to you in your life as a kitchen match.

_____

_____

_____

_____

_____

Common Threads

These trios of words have something in common. Write your one-word answer on
the line.

Examples: dance, stairs, ladder   <u>steps</u>

car, elephant, tree   <u>trunk</u>

1. baseball, unions, bowling   _____

2. horses, brakes, closets   _____

3. ruler, shoe, hill   _____

4. mouth, comb, fairy   _____

5. face, needle, hurricane   _____

6. hearth, fly, gun   _____

7. music, soap, saloon   _____

8. bands, cows, cars   _____

9. robin, theater stage, pilot   _____

10. finger, boxing, bathtub   _____

11. dog, pillow, clock   _____

12. car trunk, cards, rabbits   _____

Above or Below?

The first 25 letters of the alphabet make up the puzzle on this page. Some of the letters are placed above the line, some below. Figure out the pattern. Then write the letter Z where it belongs.

A		EF	HI	KLMN		T	VWXY
BC		G	J		OPQRS	U	
D							

Why does the Z belong where you placed it?

_____

_____

Now make up your own alphabet puzzle below. Ask a friend to solve it.

Traditional Riddles

These riddles have been stumping puzzlers for years. See if you can solve them.

1. An explorer walked one mile due south, one mile due east, and then one mile due north. Just as she realized she was right back where she started, she was attacked by a bear. What color was the bear? How do you know?

   _____

   _____

   _____

2. Nan and Jan are twins. How can Nan stand behind Jan and Jan stand behind Nan at the same time?

   _____

   _____

   _____

3. In her dresser drawer, Lelia has 16 blue socks and 16 black socks. The lights are out, and she can't see which is which. How many socks will she have to remove from the drawer to be sure she has a matching pair?

   _____

   _____

   _____

Hink Pinks

Hink pinks are rhyming pairs of words. Beside each definition, write a hink pink that fits.

Example: A giant boar is a   <u>big pig.</u>

1. An overweight feline is a _____.

2. A sugary snack is a _____.

3. A slippery hen is a _____.

4. A canine kiss is a _____.

5. A rotten potato is a _____.

6. An unusual rabbit is a _____.

7. An untamed minor is a _____.

Hinkie pinkies have two syllables in each word. Try to solve these.

8. A funny cat is a _____.

9. A monster movie is a _____.

10. A fortunate mallard is a _____.

11. A copper teapot is a _____.

12. A wedding limousine is a _____.

Letter Soup

An *anagram* is a word or phrase made by rearranging the letters of another word or phrase. Write anagram word pairs to fit each description. (You may use a dictionary.)

Example: An adored book is a   <u>dear read.</u>

1. A flower in pain is a _____.

2. Extra Bartlett fruits are _____.

3. A nasty moniker is a _____.

4. A nightmare with guns is an _____.

5. A partner on an athletic squad is a _____.

6. A tardy story is a _____.

7. A gooey, greasy grin is a _____.

8. A tire swap is a _____.

_____

Scratch Pad—Scribble here

Don't Bug Me

The science teacher gave a pop quiz on insects. Below are five students' answers.

Jack	Jill	Toh
1. firefly	1. firefly	1. firefly
2. flea	2. flea	2. tick
3. bumblebee	3. bumblebee	3. wasp
4. fire ant	4. fire ant	4. beetle
5. grasshopper	5. moth	5. moth

Minnie	Lee
1. ladybug	1. ladybug
2. tick	2. tick
3. bumblebee	3. bumblebee
4. beetle	4. beetle
5. grasshopper	5. moth

Jack got a better grade than Jill. Toh got more right than Minnie. Lee got only two correct, but which ones?

What was the correct answer to each question?

1. _____

2. _____

3. _____

4. _____

5. _____

Word Associations

Fill in words that are associated with the word above and that begin with the letter listed. Make an unbroken chain of word associations.

Example: Baby

B   <u>bottle</u>

M   <u>milk</u>

C   <u>cow</u>

Bull

1. Hammer

    N _____

    F _____

    H _____

    B _____

    Basket

2. Summer

    W _____

    S _____

    W _____

    B _____

    Coal

3. Tooth

    D _____

    D _____

    M _____

    G _____

    Ring

4. Bird

    N _____

    E _____

    B _____

    K _____

    Stove

5. Rain

    S _____

    T _____

    B _____

    S _____

    Bubbles

Answer Key

Word Squares (page 2)

Answers will vary. Good problem solvers will try lots of combinations to glean as many points as possible. One example of answers that earn the maximum 15 points would be: saxophone, drums, trombone, music, guitar

A Picture Is Worth at Least a Couple of Words (page 3)

Man overboard; six feet underground; snake in the grass; falling in love; overstuffed chair. Other answers will vary, but students should transform well-known sayings into visual images that their classmates can decipher.

Common Knowledge (page 4)

Encourage fluency of associations, so students don't get stuck on this one. Brainstorming as many words as possible associated with each word will help. Answers are:

2. ice	4. net	6. dips	8. decks	10. bucks
3. strike	5. track	7. diamond	9. swing	

Double Trouble (page 5)

Context clues form the basis for figuring out the homophone pairs.

1. whole hole	6. wood would	11. foul fowl
2. heel heal	7. dear deer	12. sail sale
3. horse hoarse	8. pale pail	13. lone loan
4. minor miner	9. nose knows	14. patience, patients
5. we'd weed	10. ate eight	15. to two, too

Decomposition (page 6)

Students who have a difficult time visualizing the new words can practice by writing each letter on a square of paper and moving the squares around. Answers are:

barbed, bread, read, ade, ad, a

salmon, mason (or moans), moan, man, an, a

pastry, strap, part, tap, at, a

planter, planet, plane, plan, pan, an, a

steamer, stream (or master), steam (or teams), team (or meat or tame), mat, at, a
rasping, spring, grins, sing, gin, in, I

You've Got a Pal in Palindrome (page 7)

Examples of acceptable words are:

a	an	am	ad	are
alone	aid	air	aim	ale
ape	pal	paler	pain	pail
pale	pad	pair	pin	pod
plain	plane	rail	par	pan
prim	paid	pore	prim	line
lid	lap	lip	lair	lone
lad	load	lope	lane	lair
laid	lain	laden	lame	limp
lore	lined	loped	lime	lied
loner	no	nope	nail	name
nor	nod	nape	near	ear
dip	dim	die	din	dare
dale	dial	dear	dam	dream
drape	drop	dram	dome	read
rod	rode	road	ram	rim
real	rid	rap	rip	rope
dope	reap	rape	renail	me
mar	mad	map	mop	mope
mile	mail	male	more	modern
peal	meal	made	maid	merlin
paler	diner	liner	mailer	deal

More Word Pictures (page 8)

Have fun guessing student word pictures. The answers follow.

An eye for an eye; a tooth for a tooth.
The pen is mightier than the sword.
Don't split hairs.
Keeping up with the Joneses
She's over the hill.
Buckle up for safety.
Working hand in hand

Feeling under the weather
Divide and conquer.

Alice, Lice, Lie (page 9)

Doublets may be worked from either word.

1. warm, worm, word, cord, cold
2. lose, lone, line, fine, find
3. more, lore, lose, loss, less
4. none, done, dome, some
5. hard, hare, bare, bore, sore, sort, soft
6. show, stow, stew, stem, seem, seam, seal, sell, tell

Word Bits (page 10)

1. cattle
2. walnut
3. muffin
4. purple
5. legend
6. squall
7. lawyer
8. chisel
9. finger
10. eleven
11. violin
12. nickel
13. desert
14. regret
15. turkey

Word Chains (page 11)

1. basket, kettle
2. collar, larger
3. letter, terror
4. pepper, perish
5. mascot, cotton
6. sudden, dental
7. rascal, calico
8. pucker, kernel
9. harbor, border
10. weapon, ponder

Not Baaad! (page 12)

Examples include:

toot	whisper	buzz	zap	tweet	caw	peep
honk	woof	slap	plunk	shush	gobble	croak
hiss	meow	clunk	fizzle	groan	hum	crunch
plop	baa	burst	click	moan	neigh	psst
splat	moo	flick	cluck	roar	growl	click
screech	whistle	pow	tinkle	bleat	quack	squawk

Word Follow-ups (page 13)

1. shell	3. ship	5. spot	7. wall	9. cracker
2. side	4. way	6. cat	8. house	10. bag

Vocabulary Stretches (page 14)

These are just some of the many possible answers:

<u>Synonyms for SAID:</u> retorted, explained, elaborated, informed, related, narrated, revealed, spoke, insisted, remarked, uttered, expressed, voiced, verbalized, pronounced, conveyed, muttered, mumbled, exclaimed, yelled, snarled, grunted, bellowed, whined, stammered, drawled, announced

<u>Synonyms for WALK:</u> plod, go, move, creep, inch, poke, toddle, shuffle, trot, dawdle, traipse, mosey, trudge, skedaddle, scuttle, lope, hasten, budge, stir, travel, amble, hobble, stagger, roam, journey, saunter, amble, meander, perambulate, waddle, promenade, slog

<u>EMOTION words:</u> angry, mad, furious, enraged, excited, wrathful, indignant, exasperated, tranquil, peaceful, unruffled, detached, aloof, eager, enthusiastic, delighted, fearful, dismayed, alarmed, horrified, apprehensive, happy, pleased, contented, joyful, cheerful, delighted, ecstatic, jubilant, gratified, outraged, glad, unhappy, miserable, uncomfortable, wretched, gloomy, heartbroken, glum, melancholy, depressed, afraid, frightened, stunned

A-Maze-Ing (page 15)

Students may give long, detailed instructions, turn by turn, but the simpler way to organize and describe getting through the maze is something like this:

As you enter, put out your left hand and touch the wall. Follow that wall, no matter how it turns and twists, and you will come out safely.

Nab the Kidnapper! (page 17)

To solve this story, students will need to distinguish relevant from irrelevant information. We know that Richie was blindfolded and never saw the kidnapper. Therefore, Johnny, the first suspect, knew he was risking nothing by asking to be put into a line-up. Johnny is the dastardly kidnapper.

The Fibber (page 18)

Barney must have said or done something to show the detective he was involved. If you go over his statement carefully, you will find a contradiction. The crowbar belonged in the garage. Yet Barney stated that the garage was locked and the burglars had not gone in there. Therefore, he must have gotten the crowbar out himself.

The Cookie Monster (page 19)

One way to solve this sort of logic problem is to set up a grid showing all the yes-no possibilities. Remember, only one statement is true. If Margaret's statement is correct, then Debbie's and Katherine's must be correct as well, and that can't be, because there is only one true statement. If Susan's or Katherine's statement is true, then Debbie's statement is also true, and that can't be, because there is only one true statement. If Debbie's statement is true, either Susan or Katherine is also telling the truth, which can't be. Therefore, Katherine's statement is true. She did not take the cookies. If her statement is true, all the other statements must be false, which means that Debbie took the cookies.

The Motorcycle in the Dell (page 20)

It's essential to analyze the details to solve this story. It's not the person, but the person's motorcycle that will win or lose the race. Therefore, the father must have told the younger boy to race off on his brother's cycle, not his own.

A Crabby Cabby (page 21)

There may be a number of possible solutions to this one. The most elegant, however, is that the traveler realized he had told the cabby where he wanted to go—the airport—and the cabby drove him straight there. Therefore, the cabby could hear.

Food Chain Farmer (page 22)

The farmer carries the chicken across first, leaving the fox and the corn behind. Then he carries the corn across and leaves it but brings the chicken back with him. He drops off the chicken and rows the fox across, leaving it with the corn again. Finally, he goes back and gets the chicken.

Taradiddle (page 23)

The bird in the tree would say yes in any case. If it really was a Veritee, it would have to say yes to be truthful. If it was not a Veritee, it would have to tell a whopper and say that it was. Therefore, since the bird on the ground said the other would say yes, he must be telling the truth. They can't both be lying. The bird in the tree is a Whopper. The bird on the ground is the Veritee.

Meow Times Four (page 24)

This puzzle shows how, when one strategy is confusing, another might be quite simple. It's easy to get confused reading the description. But once you draw what you are reading, the solution is obvious. Pudge's cage is next to Mr. Kitty's.

The Draggin' Dragons (page 25)

Drawing a grid and using X's and O's makes this one easier to sort out. We are told that Flame, Smoke and Grumpy are not mice. Therefore Fangs must be the mouse. We are also told that if Flame is not a kitten, then Fangs is not a mouse. But we know Fangs *is* a mouse; therefore, Flame must be a kitten. We are told Flame, Fangs, and Grumpy are not fleas. Therefore, Smoke must be. If we know Flame is a kitten and Fangs is a mouse and Smoke is a flea, then Grumpy must be the gerbil.

Nightmare (page 26)

There may be a number of plausible solutions to this one. But the traditional answer is that the guard was on the night shift. He had his nightmare while asleep on duty!

What If??? (page 28)

Encourage students to share a variety of answers. Possibilities might include these: there would be more vegetarians; we would know more about flight from birds; perhaps there would be insect spies; pets would probably be much better treated; pets would be chosen more on the basis of personality than of looks; few people could boil lobsters alive anymore; whales could tell us the secrets of the seas; etc.

Not to Decide Is to Decide (page 29)

Answers will vary. Possibilities follow.

1. *pro:* If circumstances change, the person will have the most information possible to make a decision.
   con: Sometimes making a decision early means you have more chances to enjoy the fruits of that decision.
2. *pro:* This person is likely to be happier or less anxious than people who agonize over their decisions.
   con: People like this rarely challenge themselves and so rarely feel great satisfaction in the consequences of a decision.
3. *pro:* Someone who looks so carefully at all sides is apt to make very informed decisions.
   con: Making everything so complicated can make one indecisive or anxious.
4. *pro:* Sometimes other people have valuable information to offer.
   con: If you always follow what other people think, you never get to know your own mind or own your decisions.
5. *pro:* This person doesn't waste time wavering.
   con: If you make a decision too quickly, you might not take all the factors into account.

Look out Below! (page 30)

Students may take one of two tacks when completing this page. Their responses to the aliens might show themselves as aggressive and able to defend themselves or they might show that we are friendly and peace loving. Sharing answers and discussing them would be fun and enlightening.

Forever (page 31)

Answers will vary, but students will need to take the time to analyze and evaluate their own interests and talents to create a satisfying list. They will also need to look ahead and predict their needs in years to come. Since none of us knows what it might be like to live forever, some students may also choose to include a means to commit suicide. Hearing one another's lists is part of the benefit of completing this activity.

Recycle Challenge (page 32)

You may want to discuss ways to reuse the items listed individually as a one-minute warm-up. Student creations will vary. Accept both serious and silly but creative reactions.

Dictionary Madness (page 33)

A wide variety of answers is inevitable on this page. Some students may react to the sounds of the words; others might make other associations as they invent their words and definitions. Encourage students to share their thought processes.

Shrink and Stretch (page 34)

Answers will vary. For example, a tiny washing machine can serve as a finger bowl at fancy meals, wash jewelry, or serve as a cat's play toy. You may want to allot just seven minutes to this activity and save three minutes for sharing answers. Having little time will force students to increase their flow of creative ideas. Hearing one another's responses to this activity may help students stretch their creativity because it will illustrate how many different ideas there are for any one invention.

Peek Pocket (page 35)

The idea here is to encourage the flow of creative ideas. If students get stumped, encourage them to keep writing—even the silliest ideas they can think of—or assign them to partners and let them brainstorm together. Sharing their responses can help them see the wide range creative ideas can cover.

Eggsactly (page 36)

Inventions should take the fragility of eggs into account. Have as many students share their responses as time permits. Do they all share a single approach? Try to think of a completely different principle on which to base the invention and share it with the class.

Peanut Butter Is the Center of the Universe (page 37)

Making connections and associations is the goal here. Accept even the wildest answers, as long as students can explain a connection. Answers will vary. Possibilities follow.

1. Fish have a strong smell, and so does peanut butter.
2. Rugs are spread on the floor; peanut butter is spread on bread.
3. Socks coat our feet, and peanut butter coats our tongues.
4. Chickadees are one of the most common birds, and peanut butter is one of the most common foods.
5. A house would be nothing without walls, and a peanut butter sandwich would be nothing without peanut butter.
6. Eggs have shells, and so do the peanuts that peanut butter comes from.
7. Dogs are man's best friend, and peanut butter is kid's best food.

8. If you spread chunky peanut butter on a table, it might look a bit like the surface of the moon.
9. Worms live underground, and peanuts grow underground.
10. Stamps are sticky, and so is peanut butter.

What Kind of Animal Is Your Uncle? (page 38)

Metaphor is one of the cornerstones of creativity. Here, students create metaphors about a person. Answers will vary but should show that students are making comparisons and connections.

No Lion Around (page 39)

Encourage students to have fun brainstorming lots of different practical and silly approaches to this problem. If possible, set aside a few minutes for sharing answers.

Imogene Ashun's Quotations (page 40)

Answers should vary wildly but somehow connect the meaning of the quotation with the imaginary speaker. The real authors are:

1. Winston Churchill
2. Martin Luther King
3. Lao-tze
4. Groucho Marx
5. Pablo Neruda
6. Theodore Roosevelt
7. George Orwell
8. Rudyard Kipling

Splat the Blats (page 41)

Students may work individually or in pairs to solve the Blands' problem. Answers should vary but might include a portable smoky fire, hats with batting hands, or giant air machines, for example. Students can practice their public speaking by pretending to try to sell their inventions to the class.

A Pungent Problem (page 42)

Student solutions may involve a method for releasing the skunk from more than five feet away or perhaps protective clothing and mask to render the skunk's spray harmless. According to some sources, covering the trap with a blanket so the skunk cannot see prevents it from spraying.

You Name It (page 43)

Punning is a form of humor that requires analyzing language and making connections. Answers will vary, of course. You may want to consider offering extra points to anyone who can make a pun from his or her own name.

Hidden Animals (page 45)

The hidden animal is a hen. The best strategy might be to start with one or two answers you are sure of and find the common word "hen" before trying to fill in the other words.

1. ashen
2. kitchen
3. lichen
4. then
5. chenille
6. Athens
7. heathen
8. henna

Bonus: Students who think it through might realize that either a regular or a rhyming dictionary can be a helpful tool to find as many cat words as possible. Answers might include cat, catalog, catastrophe, cataclysm, cataclysmic, catacomb, catalpa, catapult, cataract, catch, catcher, category, caterpillar, cathedral, ducat, kitcat, muscat, scat, magnificat, polecat, etc.

Bow Wow Wower (page 46)

Emily – collie – Ralph
Brandon – terrier – Sam
Bret – spaniel – Fiddle
Sandy – basset – Bruiser
Rosie – poodle – Snooky

How to figure it out: Bret's dog is not called Bruiser (clue 1) or Ralph (clue 2). Clue 5 shows he's not Snooky or Sam, so he must be Fiddle. That means Brandon's dog must be Sam, because clue 3 says one of them owns that dog. Clue 3 shows Bret's dog Fiddle must be a spaniel. Snooky is not Sandy's dog (clue 1) or Emily's (clue 4), so she must be Rosie's. Since Snooky is not a collie (clue 5) or a basset (clue 4), she must be a poodle. Clue 2 tells us Ralph is not Sandy's dog, so Bruiser is, which means Ralph must be Emily's. Brandon's dog is not a basset (clue 4) or a collie (clue 5), so it is a terrier. Ralph is not a basset either (clue 4), so he is a collie and Bruiser is the basset.

A Problem with Poetry (page 47)

Many words might be acceptable. Sharing reasoning would be of value here. Emily Dickinson's words are hope (Poem 1) and possibility (Poem 2).

Proverbial Wisdom (page 48)

The easiest way to crack this code is to look at the letter that stands alone. In our language, such a letter is almost always an A or an I. In this case, it is an A, and all the letters of the alphabet have been substituted for one another backwards, so that a Z is actually an A, a Y is actually a B, an X is actually a C, and so on. The proverb reads: "A wise man may change his mind; a fool, never."

New World (page 49)

Students must consider the possible consequences of an antiaging pill and use their judgment to evaluate how the pill might be regulated. Answers will vary. Encourage students to share their reasoning. Point out how their decisions are based on certain core values they may not even be aware of.

Egghead Nursery Rhymes (page 50)

The nursery rhyme is "Three Blind Mice." Student versions will vary but should show a critical and creative use of vocabulary.

Super Egghead Proverbs (page 51)

1. Every cloud has a silver lining.
2. It is an ill wind that blows no good.
3. What is sauce for the goose is sauce for the gander.
4. April showers bring May flowers.
5. Pride goeth before a fall.
6. A friend in need is a friend indeed.
7. If you lie down with dogs, you will get up with fleas.
8. Home is where the heart is.
9. Beauty is skin deep.
10. Where there's smoke, there's fire.

Unmentionables (page 52)

Student answers will vary. You may want to remind students that authors often hint at events without stating them so that readers can infer what is happening.

Burn, Baby, Burn (page 53)

Answers will vary. If students have difficulty imagining reasons why they might want to be lit, here are some possibilities:

1. Matches were meant to be lit; this will fulfill your destiny.
2. It would be boring beyond belief to lie around in a matchbox for years and years.
3. If there is such a thing as reincarnation, you'd have a chance to be reborn as something else.
4. Being lit, you might be performing a good deed for someone.
5. Being lit is more exciting than lying around.

Common Threads (page 54)

1. strikes	4. teeth	7. bars	10. rings
2. shoes	5. eye	8. horns	11. tick
3. foot	6. fire	9. wings	12. jack

Above or Below? (page 55)

The pattern here is quite simple: The letters above the line are all straight lines, while the letters below the line have curves. The Z belongs above the line.

Traditional Riddles (page 56)

1. White. It has to be a polar bear, because the explorer must be at the North Pole to walk south, east, and north to arrive back at her starting point.
2. Nan and Jan can stand back to back.
3. Three. Either she'll have all the same color, so there'll be at least one matching pair, or two of one color and one of another, so she'll still have a matching pair.

Hink Pinks (page 57)

1. fat cat
2. sweet treat
3. slick chick
4. pooch smooch
5. dud spud
6. rare hare
7. wild child
8. witty kitty
9. creature feature
10. lucky ducky
11. metal kettle
12. marriage carriage

Letter Soup (page 58)

1. sore rose
2. spare pears
3. mean name
4. armed dream
5. teammate
6. late tale
7. slime smile
8. tread trade

Don't Bug Me (page 59)

1. firefly
2. tick
3. wasp
4. beetle
5. grasshopper

The trick to this puzzle is not to get caught up in the details and to compare answers among the test takers. Jack and Jill have the same answers to all questions except number 5. Since Jack had a better grade than Jill, grasshopper must be the correct answer to question 5. That means Toh got number 5 wrong, while Minnie got it right. Since Toh did better than Minnie, Minnie had to have at least two wrong answers and Toh has to have at least three right. Lee, on the other hand, got only two right. Since tick and beetle are the only two answers he has in common with Toh, they must be Lee's two correct answers, making all Lee's other answers incorrect.

Word Associations (page 60)

Student answers may vary, as long as each word in the chain is associated somehow with the one before and after it. Possible answers follow.

1. hammer, nail, finger, hand, ball, basket
2. summer, winter, snow, white, black, coal
3. tooth, dentist, drill, mine, gold, ring
4. bird, nest, eggs, breakfast, kitchen, stove
5. rain, shower, tub, bath, soap, bubbles

Share Your Bright Ideas

We want to hear from you!

Your name_____Date_____

School name_____

School address_____

City _____State _____Zip_____Phone number (_____)_____

Grade level(s) taught_____Subject area(s) taught_____

Where did you purchase this publication?_____

In what month do you purchase a majority of your supplements?_____

What moneys were used to purchase this product?

_____School supplemental budget   _____Federal/state funding   _____Personal

Please "grade" this Walch publication in the following areas:

	A	B	C	D
Quality of service you received when purchasing	A	B	C	D
Ease of use	A	B	C	D
Quality of content	A	B	C	D
Page layout	A	B	C	D
Organization of material	A	B	C	D
Suitability for grade level	A	B	C	D
Instructional value	A	B	C	D

COMMENTS:_____

_____

What specific supplemental materials would help you meet your current—or future—instructional needs?

_____

Have you used other Walch publications? If so, which ones?_____

May we use your comments in upcoming communications?   _____Yes   _____No

Please **FAX** this completed form to **888-991-5755**, or mail it to

Customer Service, Walch Publishing, P. O. Box 658, Portland, ME 04104-0658

We will send you a **FREE GIFT** in appreciation of your feedback. **THANK YOU!**